What I Wish to Say Aloud

Julia Small

BookLeaf
Publishing

India | USA | UK

Presentation by *BookLeaf Publishing*

Web: www.bookleafpub.com

E-mail: info@bookleafpub.com

ISBN : 9789357446976

First edition 2021

DEDICATION

To all the powerful women who feel powerful things.

ACKNOWLEDGEMENT

A special thank you to the women who surround me in our creative writing class. You grant me the permission to express myself and the inspiration to chase my dreams.

PREFACE

Poetry is a funny thing in that it's completely subjective. I do not wish to explain away your pain; instead, I fearlessly show my own. This book is yours, and I encourage you to fill the empty space with your thoughts. These pages cannot judge you; let them relieve the weight you've been carrying.

Giver

Who am I if not the image you've created?
To lend my soul to take on the traits you require.
Accept the pieces of me until I have nothing left,
a simple offering of understanding greater than
I'd ever grant myself.
Take the advice I'll never follow,
find healing in my hollow words.
Tell me everything and leave out no details.
Stand on your own,
and leave me with crutches.

Her Eyes

Crystal blue dimming to a fog grey.
The light is fading, it's going out.
Her eyes.
Have seen so much.
Innocence of her perception of life is cold.
Grasping on to the last bit of hope,
Her eyes.
Overwhelmed with fear,
Screaming out to the world for help.
She lays down one last time,
Will her eyes open once more?

Love of the Past

Love is a funny thing isn't it?
I can't describe my love for you,
or where it came from.
What I can say is I know I've loved you before a
thousand lifetimes worth.
Cobblestone streets,
bar fights of olden days,
dying street lamps on a dusty corner.
They say love is timeless and I know that now,
what I feel, people write songs and movies
about.
That grip you at your throat, make your knees
weak kind of love,
what I feel is utterly breathless.
Therefore I can confidently say I have loved you
before.

Touch

Touch me she said as tears ran down her face,
what she wanted was a glimpse of what she
knew she could never have.
She sought comfort in evil's embrace,
it didn't matter who it came from, so long as it
was physical.
She learned quickly that touch isn't always
worth it.
Hands have the ability to heal, but an undeniable
power to break.
So why bother knowing the alternative?
Because all she ever wanted was to be enough.
Enough to stay, enough to make it, and most of
all enough to be loved.
To feel the weightlessness of an embrace,
to know at that moment, everything would be
okay.
That time would graciously slow to allow her to
feel every second in the darkest corners of her
mind,
a simple reminder that life had something to
offer her.

Rouge

You see a scar,
I choose to believe they are simple triumphs,
reminders of what I've overcome,
a testament to the battles I've won,
the woman I'm turning into.
I am not hopeless, I never have been.
I'm a lost soul on a mission to find my purpose,
a place in the world where I can experience pure
bliss,
an explanation to suffering so profoundly.
Reparation for all that I am.
What I seek is a lifetime of laughter, love, and
satisfaction.
Until that time comes, I will take it out on
myself.

To Myself

I don't like you.
Not like I used to,
I no longer wake up refreshed to be in your
body,
I don't want to brush your hair, or put on your
makeup.
You aren't who I remember.
You've changed, and I don't like it.

The Painter

Her eyes tell a million stories, just like her art.
She paints what thousands dream of feeling,
but who is the girl behind the art?
They say creativity comes from a place of
emotional struggle,
but she would never show it on her face.
Her hands have the ability to bring dreams to
fruition, and figures to life.
With each brushstroke, she covers up the stories
of the past.
But what is art if not subjective?
Others find beauty in tragic tales and she knows
this.
What she brings to the world, is an innocent
light.
An attempt to tell a story.
If only artists were valued as highly as
rocketeers.

Grieving the Living

You're here,
but it's not the same.
You smile,
and it's no longer because of me.
You're completely satisfied without me.
You don't want to hear about my day,
or waste a moment on simple niceties.
You breathe,
but so far from me it doesn't feel real.

Pretty Little Lies

Don't tell me anything unless you mean it.
I do not wish to be tangled in your lies,
clinging to your words,
tirelessly wishing to believe what you say.
I cannot change to fit your narrative,
contorting to accept impermanence in your life.

Wash you away

She sat in the shower,
scrubbing away every single trace you had on
her.
As the water poured down her face,
the water mixed,
with streams of salted tears.
You came and you fixed,
but in the end you became one of her fears.

Listen

Tell me my mind is beautiful and not my body.
Tell me the pleasure you get from our
conversations and not the thought of being
inside me.
Validate me for who I am and not what I can do
for you.
My being is not a playground,
and my time isn't yours to waste.

Not Today

I still can't conjure you a villain.
Maybe that says something about me,
my ability to move on,
willingness to accept udder defeat.
You had me believe my pain was a fault of my
own,
that in a fucked up way I deserved what
happened.
To you I was a plaything, an entity to take your
deep suffering out on.
I felt lucky to be that person for you,
look where that got me.
You taught me that I didn't deserve love or hope,
that I was unworthy of knowing what it's like to
have someone so invested in me it makes them
dizzy,
that effortless love that is undeniably hard to
come by.
You taught me what it's like to be you, to suffer
in silence.
Shutting out anyone who cared, you didn't want
to believe your pain was real,
so I ignored mine.
What you failed to realize is the pain that ended
up contorting your views,

only made me stronger.
You hurt me,
but I got the final say.

Old Sole

She's the pair of shoes in the back of your closet.
The ones you never reach for,
collecting dust as if they never carried you.
Holes and dirt tell the stories you no longer wish
to remember.
You deleted the pictures with them because they
no longer matched your aesthetic.
Part of you needs to remember,
so they sit as they always have,
waiting for the day you'll allow them to service
you once more.

To Those I Love More Than Myself

In your darkest days,
let me lead you home.
Question everything,
knowing I'll never stop searching for the answer.
In the mirror,
recite the words from my mouth.
Grasp opportunities as if I'm guiding your hand.
And when night falls,
appreciate the breeze and the constellations as I
would.
Find joy,
and promise to never stop chasing that feeling.
Live fully, and graciously accept love.
Treat yourself with the care you know I'd give,
I find solace in knowing you'd do the same for
me.

Don't Speak

Don't tell me you care about me,
I can't let another person down.
I don't want to hear how strong you think I am,
how resilient my being is.
Let me cradle my heart and nurse my pain.
I don't need to be fixed,
give me the silence I deserve.

Puppeteer

Sprout wings from my back,
but tell me not to fly.
Harness me to the ground,
as if I never yearned to be amongst the clouds.
Inspire me to speak,
yet celebrate my silence.
Seek the comfort from me,
you'll never repay.
When I feel better,
remind me it's only because of you.
I'll always remember,
I'm yours to destroy.

Phone Cord

Don't pick up the phone.
You can't listen to another emotionless apology,
another excuse for not being there.
One more reason to believe you were right all
along.
Don't let him in once more,
no one enjoys a conversation with a ghost.

Don't Stop

Keep driving she said,
until we find somewhere where the rear view
mirror no longer shows this place.
Let us rewrite our stories,
where a room can't swallow us whole,
and the memories can't reach us.
Reliving the same day shall be a distant memory.

Rebirth

Grant me the choice to be someone else,
to relish in the problems they face.
The control to live out their potential,
a driving force to never give up.
To them,
I promise to never falter.

Enough

I will not question my worth when someone
leaves,
rather rejoice in the fact I was so profoundly
worthy they couldn't handle it.

Grow

Oh how I wish it could always smell of rain.
Envelop me in the rich earthy tones,
watch me grow from the ground,
soaking up the skies offering.
I will not fear emerging from the dirt,
let my only reliance be on the sun.
Appreciate my budding flowers in the spring,
and when the seasons change,
no longer permitting my stay,
pray for my return.